MW01248257

NLP

Utilize The Potential Of Neuro-Linguistic Programming
In Order To Enhance And Elevate Your Confidence And
Communication Proficiency

*(Transformational Strategies For Achieving Personal And
Professional Excellence)*

Pawel Robins

TABLE OF CONTENT

The Basics Of NLP 1

The N.L.P. Analysis Of Intrapersonal Communication 7

The Need For Control 26

Cognitive Processes And Prevalent Conditioning During The Formative Years 41

NLP Methods And Techniques..............................69

Principles Of Interpreting Human Behavior. 128

Utilizing Optimistic Mental Imagery For Extraordinary Achievement 139

Applications Of Nlp..148

NLP Applications In Professional, Parental, And Interpersonal Contexts 163

The Basics Of NLP

NLP, also known as Neuro-Linguistic Programming, pertains to the three fundamental elements that determine the human experience. The aforementioned elements consist of neurology, language, and programming. Neurology refers to the intricate neurological system within the human body, encompassing its vital role in regulating various physiological processes. The use of language has a profound impact on individuals' interactions and communication with their fellow human beings. Programming influences the cognitive frameworks that individuals employ to construct their understanding or interpretation of the world. The primary function of NLP is to incorporate and combine these three components. This statement elucidates the fundamental correlation between the cognitive processes of the mind and language, wherein this association significantly influences the physical and behavioral aspects of programming.

Fundamental Suppositions of NLP

All the techniques and models employed in natural language processing (NLP) stem from two underlying assumptions, namely:

The representation of the geographical area is distinct from the actual land itself.

This proposition posits that the human cognitive faculties are not invariably proficient in perceiving objective reality, and contends that individuals' encounters are invariably colored by subjectivity. The manner in which their perceptions are formed is contingent upon their past experiences, personal convictions, deeply ingrained values, and various external factors. The perceptions individuals encounter by means of their senses effectively pass through the sensory representational systems, which essentially constitute deeply subjective experiences.

Individuals' neuro-linguistic maps of reality exert influence over their behavior and shape the interpretations they assign to said behavior. They are not truly indicative of actuality. Therefore, the existence of one singular reality is nonexistent. There exists no definitive right or wrong. All aspects are aligned with individual perceptions, observed from the vantage point or standpoint of each individual. It is subject to personal perspective, indeed. Furthermore, it is not the actuality of the situation that acts as a barrier or gives rise to impediments, such as challenges or inefficient communication. The responsibility for one's perception of reality lies with oneself.

The mind and life possess inherent systemic qualities.

Systemic processes encompass intra-individual, interpersonal, and person-environment interactions. Bodies, societies, and the universe are interconnected, giving rise to an ecosystem comprised of intricate networks of systems and subsystems. These elements continually interact with one another and exert mutual influence upon each other. It is unfeasible to singularly isolate and dedicate exclusive attention to one aspect. Every component constitutes an integral part of a broader framework, such that any alteration in one element will exert an impact on the entirety of the system, even extending to the minutest subsystem. These systems operate on principles of self-organization that innately strive to attain an optimal state of homeostasis or equilibrium.

The entirety of knowledge available to humanity, encompassing fields such as ecology and ethics, has derived solely from a singularly accurate depiction or representation of the world. This is due to the inherent inability of humans to reach a consensus on any singular, definitive concept. Therefore, the objective is to develop a comprehensive map that encompasses a high level of detail; one that upholds the harmonious coexistence between humanity and the environment, both at the individual and global level. The individuals who have proven to be the most efficient are those who have skillfully constructed a comprehensive blueprint of reality, enabling them to access a wide array of credible options and viewpoints. Through the application of Natural

Language Processing (NLP), an expansive array of options becomes accessible, thereby enhancing the range of choices at your disposal. Excellence is achieved by having as many choices as possible, which only comes from getting multiple perspectives.

The N.L.P. Analysis Of Intrapersonal Communication

The content of internal communication comprises visual representations, auditory elements, and emotional expressions, following the NLP VAK Model. Identifying the sources of your tense emotions entails determining the visual and auditory stimuli that are associated with your strained disposition. As you shift your focus inward, exploring your internal perceptions of sight and sound, you may discover that you are mentally envisioning aspects related to the meal:

As you can observe, your household appears disordered upon the arrival of the guests.

A voice within oneself that states, "They will detest the meal you have prepared."

Evident signs of unease can be observed on their faces as they consume their meal.

You find yourself in solitude at your residence due to the absence of any visitors.

Etc. The reality is: It is highly probable that you were not intentionally aware of all the internal communication channels. If you are experiencing unease regarding the evening meal, it is probable that you are mentally constructing negative scenarios and consequently reacting to them on a subconscious level. Emotional tensions manifest as a result of disparate avenues of expression.

According to Neuro-Linguistic Programming, individuals are considered intact, thereby refuting the notion of brokenness. Our primary response is to an internal correspondence, irrespective of our awareness of it. In a similar vein, if you anticipate unfavorable circumstances arising at your evening gathering, you will experience a heightened state of tension. You're working impeccably.

Once you attain an awareness of your magnificent ability to create a perspective that is undesired, you can proceed to modify it. Neuro-Linguistic Programming provides an extensive repertoire of methods to modify our mindset once we acknowledge it. The alteration of internal communication in order to enhance one's well-being constitutes the programming aspect of neuro-linguistic programming (N.L.P).

Commercialization and Evaluation"
"Monetization and Examination"
"Marketization and Appraisal"
"Businessization and Analysis"
"Profitization and Validation"
"Capitalization and Review"
"Entrepreneurship and Appraisal"
"Exploitation and Assessment

In the late 1970s, the emerging field of human development had effectively transitioned into an industry, providing a platform for the dissemination and commercialization of certain concepts within the realm of N.L.P. The Esalen Institute located in Big Sur, California, stood as the central focus of this development. Perls had driven various Gestalt treatment classes at Esalen. Satir was an esteemed trailblazer, while Bateson contributed as a visiting academic. According to Bandler and Grinder, despite serving as a therapeutic modality, N.L.P. also served as a comprehensive inquiry into communication and was later adopted as a pragmatic tool for business purposes, with the claim that "if any individual is capable of achieving something, so are you." Following a significant influx of 150 students, each paying $1,000 for a ten-day workshop in Santa Cruz, California, Bandler and Grinder chose to relinquish their scholarly pursuits. They proficiently supplied renowned literary works derived from course transcripts, exemplifying the likes of Frogs into Princes, a publication that garnered sales exceeding 270,000 copies. According to court records pertaining to an intellectual property dispute between Bandler and Grinder, it has been documented that Bandler generated in excess of $800,000 in profits in the year 1980 through the sale of workshops and books.

A collective of psychotherapists and students began to adhere to the foundational works of Bandler and Grinder, leading to the emergence and dissemination of N.L.P. as both a theoretical framework and practical application. For example, Tony Robbins engaged in preparation alongside Grinder. He incorporated a few concepts derived from neuro-linguistic programming (N.L.P.) into his personal development and persuasive communication initiatives, regarding them as highly noteworthy components. Bandler made several unsuccessful attempts to exclude various groups from utilizing N.L.P. Meanwhile, the growing number of practitioners and scholars caused N.L.P. to become even more heterogeneous than it was initially. Prior to the deterioration of N.L.P., experts in logic initiated empirical testing of its theoretical foundations, revealing a dearth of empirical evidence to support the fundamental principles of N.L.P. During the 1990s, there was a lack of rigorous investigations scrutinizing the methodologies of N.L.P compared to the previous decade. Tomasz Witkowski attributes this phenomenon to a decrease in interest in the discourse, which is the result of a lack of empirical support for NLP from its proponents.

Residing within or beyond these premises? Associated or dissociated

The process of forming and severing associations is a valuable technique. When one aligns themselves with visual representations or circumstances, irrespective of their authenticity, the intensity of the sensation amplifies. When there exists a state of dissociation from a particular experience, we are able to observe ourselves within it and effectively assimilate a significant amount of information from said image.

In the context of recalling a past experience accompanied by emotions, being personally connected with it implies association, whereas observing and perceiving those emotions externally signifies dissociation from the experience.

If you happen to experience the resurgence of an unpleasant memory, it would be advisable to approach the memory in a dissociated state. There is no justification to perceive a recurrence of the past painful experience. Nevertheless, should you desire to proceed, you may adopt a perspective akin to that of observing a film from an external vantage point, thereby detaching yourself from your emotions and assuming the role of an impartial observer of your own existence. Some individuals perceive negativity in all aspects of life, whether tangible or perceived, consistently adopting an interconnected perspective. They actively engage in extensive measures to consistently experience negative emotions. Furthermore, individuals often perceive the pleasant as detached or disconnected. They have altered the manner in which they perceive things, consequently leading to the sole guarantee of depression, negativity, apprehension, and despair. If you belong to those individuals who perceive reality in such a manner, it is imperative for me to apprise you that you possess the ability to alter these patterns and engage in diametrically opposite behaviors. For it,

Perhaps you opt to perceive unpleasant memories, concerns, and even glimpses of what lies ahead. It may have been detrimental to experience them initially; there is no necessity to return to a situation that could potentially harm you again. You do not have any justification. If that was the doctrine consistently instilled within you, it is imperative for you to recalibrate your perspective, as you possess an awareness of your preferences and aversions, and an understanding of what brings about personal gratification or dissatisfaction. There is no necessity for you to derive advantages from incessant penalties.

What is the method for capturing an accurate representation of reality? Submodalities

Association and dissociation are just part of the subtle distinctions that sensory systems make. In the field of NLP, senses are conceptualized as

15

modalities, while the distinctive attributes and nuances inherent to each modality are referred to as submodalities. This signifies the sentiments we experience, perceiving these as units of significance.

Acquiring the ability to perceive memories disentangled can induce a transformation in the overall experience. Mastering the manipulation of assorted submodalities can significantly alter one's emotional response towards a certain matter, as well as impact its integration process into future cognitive processes.

Now, being afforded the chance to ascertain the submodalities of vision, one can proceed to investigate the submodalities of the remaining senses.

In the context of visuals, it pertains to aspects such as luminosity, illumination, and spatial proximity. In the domain of auditory perception, it encompasses characteristics like resonance, pitch, and amplitude. If we are discussing olfaction, it encompasses fragrances and aromas.

Similarly, in the realm of taste, it encompasses bitterness, acidity, and a blend of the two. Lastly, in the kinesthetic modality, it encompasses factors such as weight, texture, and so forth.

What would be your ideal vision for the course of your day? emotional states

Considering the effects of submodalities on all temporal dimensions, it is worth contemplating the potential enhancement and heightened allure that could be experienced in one's life by deliberately shaping the course of one's upcoming day. You would greatly facilitate your life.

The following inquiries hold substantial value and warrant consideration, should you choose to reflect upon them each morning:

What are my anticipated outcomes for the day?

What are the anticipated outcomes in the future? This provides individuals with a clear sense of orientation and objective.

Am I taking the necessary steps that directly align with my objectives? If not, it is necessary to delve further and identify areas of deficient productivity by setting clearer objectives.

Currently, am I in the role of both my own best friend and devoted follower?

Do I currently reside within my physical vessel, fully aware of my surroundings and attuned to my sensations, observing and perceiving reality, attuned to the sounds that reach my ears, and appreciating the precious experience of existence?

Perhaps you frequently contemplate the unpredictable nature of the future, however it would be prudent for you to redirect your focus towards the current moment and reflect upon the present. One can accomplish this by engaging in the practice of meditation, with an emphasis on cultivating mindfulness.

Comprehend the underlying motivation behind your actions and behaviors.

To comprehensively comprehend the workings of the mind, it is imperative that you explore and uncover your underlying motivations. An alternative approach would be to consciously distance oneself from the tendency to procrastinate. While it is possible that you are not confronted with this issue, it is worth noting that a significant number of individuals experience it due to an overwhelming number of unfinished obligations that may surpass one's expectations.

Encountering a state of immobility is an inherent aspect of one's conduct, and refraining from action can be considered its own form of engagement. Prior to engaging in such behavior, there existed a sense of motivation to partake in various activities, whether detrimental in nature such as excessive eating or smoking, succumbing to unjust demands, or simply adhering to prior agreements or assisting a beloved individual.

When investigating the causes of motivation and procrastination, direct your attention towards the preceding moments to identify the associated emotional states. By doing so, you may uncover rapid-emerging emotions that have previously gone unnoticed, yet possess the capacity to impede progress and elicit feelings of anxiety. Subsequently, return to a position preceding the act of binding. What was the cause of this occurrence befalling upon you?

The phenomenon of procrastination and the underlying factors contributing to it: Strategies for prevention and mitigation.

The crux of the issue lies in the core of the procrastination, where it becomes imperative to identify the corresponding imagery. It can pose challenges due to the mind's tendency to automatize tasks. We have been engaging in these activities for an extended period of time, to the extent that we have become unaware of our actions. Discovering the underlying factors necessitates the exercise of patience and unwavering commitment.

Adhere to these recommended guidelines:

Please decrease your speed as much as possible.

In terms of tackling challenges, it is advisable to adopt a methodical and deliberate approach, allowing your mind to operate at a slower pace. When endeavoring to locate the image or voice that halts your progression, endeavor to reduce the speed of all surrounding elements. Please refrain from contemplating the notion, as the notion arises subsequent to the visual representation.

Please participate in the process of conducting scans and adjustments. There is every justification for you to explore this opportunity, as it represents a novel skill that you can acquire. It is imperative that you allocate time for yourself. Should you analyze any task that you have postponed, it is possible that the reason for the postponement lies in your brain's inherent inclination to safeguard your well-being.

Acknowledge ambiguity for its true nature.

As you embark upon the exploration of the underlying cause of procrastination, it is likely that you are experiencing a sense of perplexity. This denotes a cipher, indicating signs of either ire or trepidation. The code protects you. Look around and you will see that there is a low feeling, which is perhaps less pleasant. Replay the visuals at a reduced speed and delineate critical junctures.

You generate a concept, attribute significance to it, imbue it with emotion, and subsequently engage in corresponding actions; for the time being, we need not concern ourselves with altering this. It is the incorrect extremity of the lever. One must strive to adopt the contrary approach, as it offers greater ease in manipulating the image or trigger, as there are no associated emotions involved, thereby mitigating risks.

Mitigate adverse auditory signals.

It would be advantageous if you were to heed the guidance of your intuition. It is plausible that the presence of such a voice could potentially impede your inclination to undertake certain tasks, thereby diminishing your self-assurance. These are remnants from our early years that, although largely resolved, continue to resonate. We consistently leave them unchanged, which is why they generate resonance. Thus, proceed inside to discern the source and direction of the auditory stimuli.

When the sound begins, promptly adjust the volume control to ensure the voice is perceived by the mind and dissipates swiftly. The subsequent phase entails encountering an unknown individual and discerning their character by perceiving the aura they exude and interpreting its meaning Now, it is imperative for you to construct a mental representation of your own persona, reflecting upon your self-perception and assessing the level of personal security you experience.

Now, one ought to affirm a profound sense of being safe, secure, and protected. You engage in positive self-talk, devoid of any negative elements.

Subsequently, the immersion of the surroundings in the rhythmic resonance of the waves serves to purify everything. One can perceive it as a repetitive motion, akin to waves rhythmically crashing upon the shore. Once that unsightly term enters the discourse, tranquility dissipates, yielding a sense of security that accompanies each subsequent wave.

Upon noticing the feelings or behaviors, promptly apply pressure to reduce speed and subsequently evaluate the consequent outcomes. If the image served as a catalyst for stimulation, modify the overall encounter by manipulating visual submodalities.

The Need For Control

Control is a subject of contention, with a multitude of individuals approaching it from diverse perspectives. It is essential for the majority of individuals to possess the capacity to regulate their lives and manipulate their surroundings. When an individual perceives themselves as having control over a given situation, it reduces the likelihood of experiencing emotions such as fear and panic.

Currently, a brief perusal of television programs demonstrates the prevalence of individuals who personify a sense of instability and lack of emotional well-being. The focal point of both reality shows revolves around individuals grappling with chemical and alcohol dependencies, consistent patterns of theft, compulsive hoarding, and a myriad of other behavioral challenges. Additionally, certain films, exemplified by "Anger Management" featuring Adam Sandler, endeavor to address profound issues relating to emotional regulation through the use of comedic elements. It is evident that there exists an apparent disparity and a call for restorative measures within society, as a substantial number of individuals remain beyond access and lack the ability to effectively navigate this prevailing situation.

For a significant number of individuals, these issues serve as the root cause of immense hardship and anguish. When individuals lack full autonomy over their lives, it may potentially result in negative consequences such as divorce, depression, and in extreme cases, suicide. Being in complete control at all times is an arduous task, but even achieving an 80 percent rate of emotional and behavioral control would be perceived as heavenly by someone experiencing a considerable absence in that area.

The Impact of Impaired Emotional and Behavioral Regulation on Your Life

There is no sentiment more profound than attaining complete cohesion and mastery over all facets of one's existence. This promotes the cultivation of contentment and enables individuals to experience a sense of respite in the face of genuine challenges. However, life is far from being uncomplicated, and there are numerous circumstances in which an individual can experience a loss of influence.

The inability to effectively control expenditures may ultimately result in both marital dissolution and financial insolvency. Failing to control one's anger can result in conflicts, confrontations, and potential legal complications.

Chemical dependencies can give rise to complications concerning employment reduction and well-being. Failing to assume control at an early stage can result in detrimental consequences that significantly undermine the quality of your life, surpassing any apprehension you may have.

Without a doubt, it will undoubtedly present challenges for both yourself and individuals in your vicinity who lack proficiency in managing their emotions and behaviors. Nervous and anxious individuals not only generate internal tension, but also amplify the stressful milieu for those in their vicinity. It is effortless to reassure oneself about abstaining from concerns, however, implementing this mindset can prove to be challenging. In truth, when one has ingrained the lifelong tendency to apprehend the multitude of potential concerns that may arise, it is invariably challenging. Making the acquisition of power a paramount objective should be a focal point in your life.

The question of acquiring power lies in determining the most effective approach to achieve it. The elucidation for the phenomenon of decay lies in the numerous attempts made, where the utilization of appropriate tools and methodologies has been insufficient. Consequently, this gives rise to a vexing cyclical process, wherein an individual engages in repetitive behavior with the anticipation of identical results. Consequently, achieving control entails modifying behaviors in a manner that yields discernible outcomes amidst the current situation.

What is Neuro-Linguistics Programming?

Neuro-Linguistic Programming (NLP) is a therapeutic modality aimed at facilitating behavioral change, which can be conducted autonomously without the direct supervision of a licensed practitioner. There is no possibility of adverse consequences in incorrectly executing the task. At most, during practice sessions when movements are performed suboptimally, no discernible impact will be observed. Its inception can be traced back to the 1970s, when novel principles were strategically implanted within the subconscious mind, aiming to explore the feasibility of elevating behavior modification strategies. Immediately from the onset, it demonstrated remarkable success.

Its increasing popularity has been observed solely in the past few decades, leading to the existence of practitioners in every state of both the United States and Canada. It is not of such complexity as to necessitate the consultation of a therapist with specific expertise, yet it is prudent to acknowledge the availability of this option should one desire it. Although the field of therapists specializing in NLP is quite limited, it may be recommended to consult with a neuro-linguist psychotherapist in order to obtain valuable insights and guidance.

It is not intended to serve as a substitute for the treatment that may be necessary in cases of chronic depression or bipolar disorder, nor is it aimed at replacing any required medication. It is advisable to seek professional advice from a doctor in order to inform them about the consideration of NLP therapy. Nevertheless, it offers numerous significant advantages, namely its inherent simplicity, versatility in execution, and the transformative impact it has on various facets of an individual's existence once consistently embraced.

What level of difficulty is involved in utilizing the NLP?

NLP's increasing popularity can be attributed to the ease and accessibility of acquiring its techniques and tools, which can be grasped with minimal exertion or hardship. The NLP-related procedures are readily comprehensible and can be readily implemented by nearly everyone without delay. There is no requirement for you to peruse or partake in specialized instructional sessions that encompass a vast amount of material. The book provides a simplified procedure to help you reset and regain control over your emotions and actions. It is essential to dedicate effort to every task, regardless of their number.

As long as you are able to allocate a few minutes each day towards the practice of NLP and maintain the convenience of having a notebook readily available, you will experience advancements. While it is advisable to establish a regular schedule for the purpose of cultivating a commendable practice of engaging in daily NLP sessions, said activities are amenable to being undertaken at any hour, irrespective of day or night. Ensure that you diligently maintain progress documentation to acknowledge your advancing efforts towards achieving the desired enhancement. In a matter of days, you will begin to observe a considerable transformation and find yourself precisely in the desired position within a matter of weeks. It renders the possibility of enduring a lengthy period of recuperation an alternative course of action that one would no longer desire to pursue.

This book contains an extensive array of techniques and tools that have been meticulously catalogued to assist individuals in achieving proficiency in the utilization of NLP. It is crucial to bear in mind that although NLP yields expedient outcomes, it should not be perceived as a readily remediable therapeutic modality. In certain circumstances, to ensure proper execution of the techniques and, naturally, to fully reap the advantages offered by NLP, it necessitates diligent and recurrent practice.

NLP Exercises

Consistently, your mind is continuously discerning sensory information. This mechanism significantly determines your perception of the world and subsequent responses to it. NLP leverages the cognitive faculty to recalibrate your actions, beliefs, and assumptions, with the aim of dissuading counterproductive tendencies, and cultivating a fresh paradigm of beliefs, behavior, and assumptions that facilitate the accomplishment of your objectives and fortify the outcomes derived from them.

NLP exercises employ each of the five senses - sight, sound, touch, taste, and smell - as means to impart novel patterns of behaviors to the mind. The sensory organs serve as conduits through which the brain establishes contact. NLP techniques are predominantly employed to improve the cohesion and regularity of an individual's existence. This process is accomplished through the reconfiguration of the manner in which cognitive faculties process incoming information. In this manner, you can employ Natural Language Processing (NLP) to facilitate personal development or enhance interpersonal connections.

Its purpose: Neuro-linguistic programming activities can be utilized in various domains of a person's life, such as circumstances that entail the elimination of an undesirable behavior and the replacement of it with a more desirable one. To alter one's perspective on something or a situation, one can exert influence over their sensory faculties. In this manner, individuals can elicit a cognitive response towards the intended emotion. In the event that you have undergone a distressing incident in your past, NLP can serve as a valuable tool to effectively manage and address the impact of that experience. Merely modify the manner in which you recollect the distressing incident. For instance, it is possible to modify the intensity of color, the luminosity of the environment, and all other aspects that contribute to the recollection of the encounter. Mitigate the intensity of these occurrences to diminish their distressing nature and guarantee that the aforementioned memory remains etched in your consciousness. You will come to realize that you need not recollect that distressing encounter in such a manner ever again.

NLP Presuppositions: Presuppositions encompass entrenched sets of beliefs that exert influence over an individual's behaviors and emotional reactions. NLP is founded upon a substantial collection of fundamental assumptions that effectively foster personal development and advancement. Certain convictions encompass aspects such as discerning legitimacy or morality, formulating presumed truths, and fostering the notion that comprehension of one's desires will facilitate their attainment.

Submodalities: In order to stimulate the desired mental response, NLP exercises employ sensory components, known as submodalities, pertaining to specific circumstances and events. The constituent elements pertaining to sensory perception in this particular scenario encompass the set of the five senses. For instance, the faculty of vision can be employed to modify an individual's perception of a particular entity or situation, encompassing, but not limited to, attributes such as hue, dimensions, and spatial proximity. Among the various auditory submodalities are sound quality, volume, and frequency range, to cite just a few examples. NLP holds potential for personal development, and in this instance, individuals can leverage submodalities to envision a prospective enjoyable encounter that can result in a transformative experience upon its fruition.

NLP Anchors for exercise: anchors will be employed in NLP to elicit emotional reactions and manipulate perceptions. In the process of visualization, the mind generates anchors to anticipate and prepare individuals for forthcoming events or circumstances, which may either be enjoyable or significant in their nature. Various forms of stimulation can serve as anchors, such as interlocking one's hands, gently biting the lips, or tapping the floor, among other possibilities. The purpose of employing these anchors is to establish a correlation between the affective responses and a forthcoming event or course of action. Throughout the process of visualization, the objective is to cultivate an optimistic environment, which ought to be maintained consistently until the actual occurrence of the event.

Cognitive Processes And Prevalent Conditioning During The Formative Years

Expanding upon our existing framework of beliefs, there exist additional complexities in comprehending our thoughts and realities. Your values and beliefs have the potential to shape your cognitive processes and form early-life conditioning; however, if you encounter unfavorable messages?

The cognitive frameworks and synaptic networks governing our perceptions of the world and ourselves, as well as our interactions with our surroundings and fellow individuals, materialize during our formative years and are subsequently reinforced over the course of our upbringing. We are under the influence of our parents, caregivers, teachers, relatives, and peers. If they display negative behavior to us as a result of not having developed a positive mindset themselves, we are likely to adopt those patterns and have limited knowledge during our childhood on how to rectify those unfavorable neural connections.

As we mature, we have the choice to enhance our understanding and acquire more constructive methods to process our emotions and perceive our reality, or we can choose to remain confined within our established thought patterns or ingrained programming, accepting that they are inherent and unalterable. By maintaining such a belief, you are perpetuating your adverse cognitive framework regarding yourself, rather than rectifying it through the utilization of accurate information or exemplary behavior.

One advantageous aspect of Neuro-Linguistic Programming is its proposition that should one be dissatisfied with their emotional response towards a particular matter, they have the ability to modify it accordingly.

You possess the capability to modify your cognitive patterns, even in cases where they appear deeply entrenched due to their formation during childhood. In subsequent chapters, you will acquire comprehensive knowledge on these topics and beyond. However, prior to delving into the subsequent chapters, it is crucial for you to discern the various manifestations of negative thought patterns and programming in your beliefs and values, as well as your attitudes and convictions.

Cognitive distortions are occasionally referred to as negative thought patterns. A thought pattern refers to any cognitive repetition that occurs on a consistent basis. This repetition may manifest as habitual actions carried out unconsciously, repetitive thoughts that contribute to unfavorable behavior, or the regular reinforcement of negative thoughts and emotions.

A few instances thereof include: -" - -" -

Making Assumptions

When individuals form presumptions regarding an individual or a circumstance, they are employing a judgmental stance in the absence of factual evidence or effective communication to ascertain the underlying causes of someone's negative behavior towards them or the reasons for the unfavorable trajectory of events. This is making hasty judgments without conducting any investigations to ascertain the accuracy of your assumptions. This situation can potentially give rise to a significant amount of distress, concern, and uncertainty, as well as create a distorted perception, particularly when interacting with others. When one harbors a pessimistic presumption about the probable outcome of a situation, they tend to persuade themselves of its veracity, despite it being merely a detrimental pattern of thinking that yields no positive results.

Catastrophizing

A calamity arises at every twist and turn, regardless of the circumstances. When one develops a cognitive tendency towards catastrophizing, they amplify or diminish their experiences, greatly exaggerating them to unrealistic extremes. This is the realm where the "What If?" inquiry holds dominion. What would ensue if the circumstances were to crumble entirely? In the event that I do not receive the promotion and subsequent salary increase, and subsequently face the unfortunate circumstance of my wife departing with our children due to financial difficulties in sustaining the mortgage, what would be the course of action? What if my life is prematurely cut short due to the impacts of global warming? The circumstances may vary from a trivial error made during one's piano lessons to the result of observing someone else's successful accomplishment in a particular endeavor.

Binary Thinking

Either this or that. It leaves no room for mediocrity, as it is characterized by either flawless execution or complete disappointment. Engaging in dichotomous thought processes occurs when we actively polarize a given situation. Complete or absolute experiences allow for limited opportunity to recognize and value the multifaceted nature and dynamic essence of any given experience. Many individuals who embody a perfectionist mindset often adhere to the notion that there can only exist one possible outcome, categorizing it as either favorable or unfavorable, accepting nothing in between.

Overgeneralizing

Over-generalization occurs when one reaches a conclusion despite having limited evidence or understanding. Therefore, in the event of an unfortunate circumstance, one might entertain the notion that because it occurred previously, it is likely to reoccur. A cascade of negative events ensues, culminating in ultimate failure. This may be classified under the category of adverse "If/Then" statements. If I have not received a response from them thus far, it is likely that they have selected another candidate for the coveted position I desire. Your thought process seems to rely heavily on speculation, lacking concrete information.

Thought-Screening

An alternative expression for this would be to refer to it as "selective perception." In this case, when an event occurs, the cognitive tendency is to selectively perceive and emphasize the negative aspects while filtering or excluding the positive and neutral aspects of the situation. It represents a narrowed perspective that significantly limits the capacity for lucidity and comprehension. This phenomenon may occur organically and in constructive manners, as it stems from our innate inclination to adhere to familiar patterns in life, thereby disregarding any potentially discomforting, unfamiliar, or unstimulating elements.

Emotional Reasoning

This is a cognitive schema that is commonly encountered by individuals due to a lack of instruction or acquisition of successful and constructive methods for assimilating and comprehending our emotional encounters. With emotional reasoning, one holds the conviction that their feelings present an exact depiction of the truth pertaining to their circumstances or reality. Instead of perceiving your emotions as the sole criterion for assessing your experiences, it would be more prudent to engage with the entirety of reality and approach it with rationality, rather than solely focusing on the emotional ramifications.

Should Talk

This phenomenon is prevalent among individuals, particularly in the form of sentences expressing obligations or expectations, commonly known as "I should" sentences. When we express the notion of obligation regarding an action or hindsight concerning a missed action, we engage in self-criticism.

Prior to engaging in any other activities today, it is imperative that I engage in physical exercise.

I ought to have composed that report by the preceding day.

I should diet.

I ought to enhance my proficiency in xyz.

I ought to have exhibited greater proficiency in xyz.

These instances merely scratch the surface of the multitude of "I should" assertions, yet they provide a glimpse into how we distort our thoughts and cultivate such a cognitive pattern to perpetuate a state of negativity or suffering within ourselves. When one habitually expresses the phrase "I should," they are implying an acknowledgement of past or potential errors, anticipating the consequent experience of shame. How do you determine the appropriate course of action and distinguish between what is permissible and what is not? Does it stem from your personal convictions and principles? Could it be attributed to the act of comparing oneself to others and observing their attitudes and behaviors?

The study of NLP offers insights into the process of reframing cognitive patterns, such as substituting the phrase "I should..." with "I could" or "I can." The significance of language lies in its role in shaping our thought patterns. The process of restructuring one's cognitive processes to comprehend individual thinking patterns and modify them with the aim of cultivating a more purposeful, self-assured, and receptive mindset towards one's encounters is merely the initial step. To increase one's prospects of achieving greater success in various domains such as career, education, and relationships, it is imperative to introspect and gain insight into the influence of one's cognitive framework on their overall life experiences.

Changing Beliefs - Part One

Altering one's convictions requires a significant investment of time and unwavering dedication, yet the rewards derived from this endeavor are truly invaluable. Ideologies serve as lenses that shape our perception of the world. They have a profound impact on our subconscious mind. The majority of these factors pertain to our perception of how adequately our needs can be fulfilled. To provide an illustration, suppose you were in the process of dashing towards a solid perimetral structure. Let us consider a scenario where there exists an entity or force in pursuit of you. With minimal cognitive deliberation, devoid of any internal dialogue, one would not necessitate substantial contemplation regarding the approach to the wall. If the height of the obstacle were sufficiently low, one would easily surmount it by means of a simple leap. In the event that the obstacle had a moderate height, you would likely exercise caution and meticulously consider the optimal placement of your hand and footing while executing your vault over it. In the event that the object assumes a chest-high position, it would be advisable to decelerate, make necessary arrangements to perform a leap, firmly grasp the object, and subsequently hoist oneself atop it, taking into account one's personal evaluation of their own leaping prowess and muscular resilience. In the event that the wall presented an insurmountable obstacle, one would inevitably decelerate upon nearing it, contemplating alternative escape routes or, conceivably, strategizing a plan of action in the event of a face-to-face encounter with one's pursuer. None of these actions would necessitate cognitive deliberation. One would perceive the wall visually, and subsequently, the brain would autonomously analyze the most suitable method for surmounting this impediment along one's trajectory. Your actions would be predicated upon your convictions regarding your physical prowess in the realms of jumping, vaulting, turning, and combat. When it comes to tangible objects, comprehending beliefs becomes more straightforward. However, when it comes to any situations involving interpersonal interactions, be it in the realm of romance, business, or any other context, our underlying principles remain unchanged although they become significantly more intricate.

To some extent, our beliefs influence our actions as we draw upon our past experiences to navigate unfamiliar circumstances. Beliefs can be conceptualized as a higher-level construct within the aforementioned process. We hold a collective conviction regarding our competence in specific scenarios. In this context, beliefs fulfill the role of mitigating the amount of cognitive effort and time required for our thinking processes. Here's another oversimplified example. Suppose you find yourself in a bar, attending to your own affairs. Two individuals a few seats away engage in physical altercation. Subsequently, a pair of additional individuals decide to participate. In a matter of moments, half of the patrons in the bar have swiftly risen from their seats, engaging in physical altercations. The emotional response you experience in this particular scenario is contingent upon your perception of your own ability to manage the situation. In the event that you possess advanced combat skills and possess ample experience in self-defense, it is conceivable that you may entertain fleeting concerns regarding the potential spillage of your beverage, albeit insignificantly so. If you lack prior experience in combat or physical exertion, or have encountered frequent instances of school abuse, you may perceive expeditious departure as the sole viable course of action.

Subconscious convictions operate on a profound level beyond surface understanding. In a given circumstance, the distinction between one's beliefs and the concept of promptly examining our memory and generating an emotional reaction is virtually indistinguishable. Divergent opinions emerge with respect to the impact of beliefs on cognition in contexts outside of one's immediate situation. However, they employ astute and covert methods to achieve their objectives. To illustrate, assuming you possess a prevailing notion that engaging in conversations with individuals in positions of authority is challenging, it shall impose constraints on your ability to envision avenues for financial gain. Your cognitive faculties effectively prevent you from envisioning any situations in which you engage in assertive communication with figures of authority as a means of generating financial gain. If you are perusing the job listings on the internet without a specific criteria in mind, you may unknowingly overlook employment opportunities that entail qualifications that you perceive as challenging to attain or acquire. Beliefs serve as a protective mechanism, shielding us from recognizing opportunities that may elicit negative emotions or emotional distress. From this perspective, restricting beliefs pose a significant threat not only due to their limiting nature, but also due to their operation at a deeply unconscious level. The extent of their concealment is such that a mere introspective examination of our minds would not suffice to uncover all of our limiting beliefs. We are obliged to proactively pursue them. This task is characterized by its arduousness, as it entails substantial emotional challenges. In the subsequent section of this chapter, our focus will be directed towards identifying and addressing these constraining beliefs. Subsequently, in the following chapter, we shall delve into the process of eliminating or modifying them.

Methods for Identifying Limiting Beliefs

We'll start with assuming there are things in life that you want, but haven't really made any serious efforts to get. Typically, these pertain to matters concerning finances, interpersonal aptitudes, or amorous affiliations. We will commence by considering the concept of increasing our earnings by a fifty percent margin. We shall proceed by making a few assumptions. One aspect to consider is the prospect of experiencing a fifty percent increase in your current income, which may bring you a considerable amount of enjoyment. It is presumed that there exists a belief that hinders you from earning an additional fifty percent income. If you held genuine conviction in your ability to achieve a fifty percent increase, you would undoubtedly take action. This is not a belief one desires to hold, rather it is an undeniable truth. That statement holds equivalent validity to your conviction in your ability to leap over that wall. When one holds a belief as true, they proceed with it in a manner devoid of conscious consideration. It's easy. Therefore, in the event that you aspire to enhance your current income by a margin of fifty percent, yet harbor a belief that obstructs your progress towards that objective, we shall commence with the following sentence stem: "

I am unable to generate a fifty percent increase in earnings due to...

And then start writing. This constitutes the challenging segment. The initial ten or twenty (or beyond) responses are unlikely to be veracious, however, they will possess an air of verisimilitude. Any response that shifts the blame onto someone other than oneself proves unproductive, as one possesses the ability to modify their own actions rather than those of others. We are seeking a response to that statement that fulfills several stipulations. One reason for this perception is that it resonates with a deeply ingrained intuition. Most significantly, it should elicit a profound and unexpected impact akin to being struck forcefully in the abdomen. One that proves challenging to articulate audibly without the manifestation of vocal tremors. This is the underlying cause for the concealment of these beliefs. Acknowledging these aspects poses an emotional burden, for they reveal deficiencies within ourselves. We circumvent acknowledging them through externalization; assuming they are the responsibility of someone else. One can conceptualize this as the predominant defense mechanism used to safeguard our self-esteem. In the event that we hold the belief that our inability to generate fifty percent higher earnings stems from a global conspiracy, it mitigates our emotional distress. Ultimately, if the world were not characterized by inherent malevolence, prosperity would be more widely bestowed upon humanity. It is for this reason that individuals find solace in collective suffering. The concept of "Misery loves company" is rooted in the tendency for individuals to seek solace in collective blame, where we come together and assign fault to others for the shared challenges we face. By engaging in this pattern of behavior, whether it pertains to financial limitations, inadequate intimate relationships, lack of acknowledgment, or any semblance of unfairness in life, we are inadvertently absolving ourselves of the accountability to rectify these circumstances. The larger our group expands, the more challenging it becomes to acknowledge that we might be responsible for the situation. This prevents us from engaging in self-reflection and taking accountability. Expressing this concept with genuine sincerity poses an immense challenge as it brings about an overwhelming surge of emotions that often leads to weeping:

I am unable to attain my desired outcome due to my insufficient skills.

What is causing such difficulty in this matter? What if we were to acknowledge our deficiency in skills, make an earnest effort to acquire those skills, and subsequently realize that we are unable to acquire them? A fundamental requirement for human contentment and joy lies in harboring aspirations for an improved tomorrow. However, should we acknowledge our inadequacy and accept that we are destined to remain inadequate, it essentially extinguishes any potential for improvement or fulfillment in our unfortunate existence. Nevertheless, there is some positive information regarding the revelation of that constraining belief (which elicits a sense of surprise and disappointment when expressed).

All Beliefs are Invalid

Unless it is a belief grounded in empirical evidence and accompanied by imminent physical evidence (such as the presence of a wall), it can be deemed unfounded. All assertions regarding our aptitude in any realm of social circumstances are unfounded. There is an abundance of variables that renders it virtually impossible to obtain a precise understanding of our true abilities in any genuine scenario.

It is preferable to exercise caution rather than risk facing negative consequences.

An enduring remnant from our ancestral era as hunter-gatherers is the inherent wiring of our brains to generate a response that upholds the notion of prioritizing caution over regret. In the bygone era, a single error could prove to be fatal. If one were to mistakenly venture into an undesirable sector of the jungle, their fate would be sealed. If one happened to communicate with an unsuitable young woman, who happened to be dating a member from an adversary tribe, the consequences would be dire. If one did not remain securely positioned within the middle of the group, the outcome would have been disastrous. Nowadays, none of those regulations are applicable. However, our primordial primate minds failed to receive the memorandum. This is precisely the reason why acknowledging our genuine limiting beliefs can be an agonizing process. We perceive them as immutable, as if we were still residing in the literal era of stone. Luckily, they are not. Similar to the other methods outlined in this guide, these techniques will require patience and time to transform, yet transform they shall.

NLP Methods And Techniques

NLP methodologies or strategies possess the ability to transform and enhance virtually any task or endeavor.

Do The Techniques Work?

Indeed, the response is affirmative. By assimilating the knowledge imparted through reading this book, you have the potential to enhance not only your personal circumstances, but also contribute to the betterment of others. Exercise caution while adhering closely to the provided instructions and be prepared to engage in some trial and error.

Presented herein are several NLP methods or techniques that you may deem worthy of acquainting yourself with, in order to enhance the quality of your daily existence.

Building Rapport

What is the Importance of Establishing Rapport?

When we establish a state of rapport with an individual, the focus is directed towards magnifying the commonalities and diminishing or downplaying the disparities that exist between us. This phenomenon is effective due to the inherent inclination of human beings to derive pleasure from being held in favorable regard.

This tendency is the underlying rationale for our inclination to be drawn towards individuals who we perceive as being similar to us. The essential foundation for effective communication lies in the act of emphasizing the similarities that exist between ourselves and others. Without establishing a sense of rapport, true communication cannot take place.

How to Gain Rapport

To achieve success in establishing rapport, it is imperative to possess the skills of observation and active listening. It is imperative to exercise considerable patience prior to pursuing one's own viewpoint.

Adaptability is the key. It is essential to attentively consider the perspective of the other individual, envisioning yourself in their situation prior to contemplating your own.

Avoid engaging in mimicry while still effectively mirroring the interlocutor's energy, speech patterns, and body language.

In the event that the individual exhibits rapid speech, endeavor to momentarily mirror their pace before gradually decelerating to assess the congruity of your respective patterns of verbal communication. Conforming to the respiratory rhythm of the other individual is the preferable approach. This phenomenon is commonly referred to as matching and mirroring. Ensure accurate and tactful imitation to avoid generating an undesired outcome.

Is the establishment of rapport in NLP primarily based on the principles of the discipline or rooted in common sense?

One could argue that this is an inherent logicality. Indeed, it is the case, however, Natural Language Processing can aid in our ability to focus on the issue at hand. By offering strategies to assist us, it serves as a reminder that we must thoroughly examine our relationships from various perspectives. Establishing a rapport constitutes an integral component of this process.

Dissociation

The term 'dissociate' denotes the act of undergoing division or separation into distinct components. Fundamentally, dissociation entails a state of detachment. It is widely acknowledged among practitioners of Natural Language Processing that deliberately maintaining a sense of detachment can be beneficial in obtaining a more comprehensive viewpoint. This is typically accomplished through the alteration, redirection, or restriction of attention; wherein one may choose to concentrate on an internal fantasy as a means of managing discomfort.

Using Association/ Dissociation

The phenomenon of dissociation holds significant value as a scientific method. When one establishes a connection, a profound experience is rekindled, evoking a spectrum of emotions. During states of dissociation, an opportunity presents itself for introspection, allowing one to impartially observe oneself and the corresponding sentiments toward the given circumstances.

When to be Dissociated

The act of disengaging or disconnecting oneself from distressing encounters or recollections can yield advantageous outcomes. By what means do you motivate yourself to undertake arduous or lengthy tasks? Observe and reflect upon your execution of the job activities, and establish a connection between the resultant outcome and the positive mental state obtained upon task completion.

Proper Techniques for Executing Dissociation

It is not arduous to respond to adverse circumstances and subsequently experience anxiety or disillusionment.

The subsequent approach can aid individuals in mitigating adverse emotions within similar circumstances. It possesses the capability to address phobias by providing an objective perspective on the situation.

Here are the steps:

Identify the specific emotion that you intend to alleviate from your being, whether it be apprehension towards creeping creatures, unease in someone's presence, or aversion to dimly lit environments.

Envision yourself as an onlooker, observing and navigating through the entirety of the situation.

Utilize the technique of mentally reenacting and reversing the sequence, followed by temporally accelerating it, subsequently repeating the process of reversing it once more.

Incorporate humorous background music into the film screening. Execute this action a minimum of 3 to 4 instances.

Now endeavor to envision the identical scenario as if it were transpiring at present. Continue executing the prescribed physical exertions until the perception of the stimulus has undergone a transformation or dissipated altogether.

Context Reframing

This is a transformative process that aims to reframe a negative occurrence into a positive experience by encouraging deep reflection on the broader context. As an illustration, if one frequently experiences discomfort when approached by a homeless individual seeking monetary assistance while strolling along the pavement, due to the belief that such individuals exhibit a lack of motivation to seek employment, an alternative perspective can be adopted. Instead, one may consider the possibility that this individual has encountered circumstances such as the loss of shelter or familial support, compelling them to reside temporarily on the streets. By broadening the scope and taking into account the likelihood that there may exist underlying causes for his homelessness and reliance on soliciting funds from unfamiliar individuals, you are engaging in the practice of context reframing. This alteration of your circumstances necessitates a revision of your constraining conviction.

The technique of reframing the context proves highly advantageous in instances characterized by sudden and uncontrollable occurrences. Gaining a different perspective on a situation can be highly advantageous in mitigating one's stress levels. The key to reframing the context lies in maintaining an open-minded attitude towards alternative possibilities beyond your initial impression.

Humor And Creativity

Typically, reframing manifests itself in the form of humor. The apparent nature of something undergoes a transformation, revealing itself to be fundamentally different than initially perceived. The circumstances lead you in one direction, while the impact line guides you in another.

Reframing needs creativity – it is about putting a normal situation or thing in a new frame that's beneficial or pleasurable.

An Alternate Perspective

NLP reframing with context derives itself from the underlying principles of NLP which posit that all behaviors carry inherent benefits under specific circumstances. By contemplating a constructive framework, one can alter their response to said conduct.

When you endeavor to guide a friend towards perceiving things from a different perspective, considering an alternate viewpoint, or contemplating other pertinent aspects, you are engaging in the process of reframing the situation with the intention of evoking a distinct response.

Outlined below are a few instances of context reframing:" "Presented here are several illustrations of context reframing:" "The following are a number of examples of context reframing:" "Herein, we offer a selection of context reframing instances:" "Provided for reference purposes are some exemplifications of context reframing:

Politicians excel at the art of changing the narrative. It appears that irrespective of the circumstances, they possess the ability to interpret events in a manner that is advantageous to themselves or detrimental to their adversaries.

It is possible that you feel a sense of frustration towards your spouse due to their decision to extend an invitation to an individual experiencing homelessness for a meal. Until the moment of your realization that said individual has abstained from consuming any sustenance for a consecutive duration of forty-eight hours.

Observe the antiquated chair residing in the depths of your basement, which has been unknowingly neglected. Upon hearing that it is a valuable antique, one is likely to perceive it in a contrasting manner without delay.

Put simply, context reframing involves examining a subject matter from an alternative standpoint. The majority of behaviors exhibit advantages or appropriateness within specific contexts.

Regain capacity for action through the implementation of Reframing techniques.

Undoubtedly, you have frequently encountered the phrase: "One can only wonder about the purpose of this!" This concise expression should not be misconstrued as an act of surrender, but rather exemplifies an individual who approaches circumstances and occurrences with a dignified equanimity. Setbacks are part of life. The effective management of crises significantly contributes to achieving success. Hence, the acquisition of resilience skills holds significant importance. In commencing promptly and performing with an elevated level of proficiency, you will enhance your ability to efficiently address forthcoming challenges.

A crucial factor in this context pertains to the cultivation of enhanced self-esteem, empowering you to effectively address and achieve your objectives. Reframing can be employed to realign things with their intended form. Karin Intveen holds the view that the process of reframing fosters an expansion of cognitive capacity, alleviates feelings of uncertainty and anger, and facilitates the restoration of one's ability to navigate situations with increased flexibility.

The inquiry, "To what purpose does it serve?", holds universal applicability in all circumstances. Considering the multitude of ongoing crises, this inquiry may appear dubious in nature. Nevertheless, the backdrop is of a more pragmatic nature. Undoubtedly, as an illustration, the termination of employment and the subsequent absence of financial resources may be perceived in this manner, yet it is equally conceivable to adopt an alternative perspective:

Now is the opportune moment to pursue alternative employment opportunities that offer improved remuneration, amiable coworkers, and enhanced scheduling flexibility.

● Currently, a unique prospect has emerged to redefine your purpose and undertake a new course of action, allowing you to achieve personal fulfillment.

● Now I am afforded the opportunity to attend to the needs and interests of other individuals and matters that hold deep personal significance to me.

Reframing can lead to the emergence of queries that elicit humorous and ironic responses, eliciting amusement upon closer examination. Although it may be considered a form of macabre wit, these instances will ignite your creativity and prompt innovative thinking. The crucial aspect lies in ensuring that you employ the technique to maintain a perpetually active state of mind.

The act of reframing does not impose any limitations on the scope of your thoughts and ideas. Thus, one can adeptly intersperse situations or challenges with a harmonious blend of vibrant hues, wit, inquiries, and even melodic compositions. Once more, as the resonating low frequencies echo through the early hours, one can envision an individual akin to a disgruntled Donald Duck, expressing incoherent mutterings and becoming visibly flushed with indignation within the realm of the imagination. Reframing confers substantial advantages by inducing relaxation not solely in the realm of cognition, but also in the entirety of one's physical being. Living becomes significantly more enjoyable and purposeful through an intensified focus on addressing and resolving challenges. If your thoughts persistently revolve around the problem in a constricted and obstinate manner, novel insights will not emerge, and resolutions will remain elusive.

The incorporation of neuro-linguistic programming techniques to facilitate the modification of attitudes and beliefs.

You may likely be acquainted with the disconcerting sensation that gradually arises in specific circumstances, inducing perspiration due to a perceived inability to cope. Perhaps now would be an opportune moment to consider reframing your thoughts and cultivating a refreshed mindset.

Your perspective relies on transformative experiences and memories that currently lie dormant within your subconscious. Even in the present day, you possess the ability to exert significant influence, a circumstance that can at times impede the progress and hinder the realization of latent capabilities. Through the utilization of neuro-linguistic programming and adopting a conducive mindset, individuals can surmount such challenges and ultimately achieve success. However, could you please illuminate the concept of Mindset? This term in the English language possesses various possible translations and interpretations. A potential generalized understanding could be articulated as follows:

- Life's philosophical principles

- Thought processes • Cognitive mindset • Mode of cognition • Mental perspective • Approach to reasoning • Framework of analysis • Philosophy of thought.

- Setting

- Attitude

- Orientation

- Attitudes

- Worldview

- Mentality

Your disposition and cognitive perspective pertaining to a particular subject exert a profound impact on your emotional state and subsequent behavior. Reciprocally, a linkage is formed by the encounters one has undergone. Not only do negative attitudes and thoughts hinder your success, but your lack of self-confidence in performing certain tasks also plays a significant role. Positive experiences in specific domains have the potential to fortify and motivate individuals as well.

Perhaps there was a circumstance in which you were required to deliver a presentation during your academic years, and found yourself at a point of impasse during its delivery. That engendered a significant amount of animosity within the academic community. This experience continues to resonate in your daily life, significantly influencing your thought patterns, as exemplified by instances such as delivering a presentation. It appears that you have harbored the notion that you possess inadequate public speaking skills, leading you to refrain from expressing your opinions or taking a stance on a specific matter in any given circumstance.

If your past experiences had been different, the act of speaking publicly today would not pose a significant challenge for you. Due to the favorable experiences you have encountered in the past, you have acquired a sense of self-assurance. You possess awareness of your capabilities and can utilize them with intention. Your mindset functions as a discerning mechanism that shapes your surroundings based on your prior experiences, while simultaneously delving into your potential opportunities. Now, it must be pondered whether adverse experiences necessarily culminate in the notion that an individual is an inept orator, as illustrated by the aforementioned scenario. Alternatively, does your disposition stem from a past encounter that has influenced your preference to avoid future instances of unpleasantness? Within your environment, there appear to be individuals who effortlessly excel in every aspect of life and exhibit unwavering confidence. You possess exceptional talent from the moment of your birth. Cease! Perhaps a certain portion of individuals possess a modicum of this ability within their genetic makeup. Perhaps you have initially developed this skill and undertaken the necessary training.

In academic research, psychologist Carol Dweck, renowned for her focus on motivational processes, has developed a compelling theoretical framework. Based on this assumption, two distinct forms of mindset can be identified. One viewpoint posits the Fixed Mindset, characterized by its unwavering and rigid nature. Conversely, an alternative perspective exists in the form of the Growth Mindset, which is characterized by its dynamic and growth-driven nature.

Individuals classified under the Fixed Mindset category frequently hold the belief that particular aptitudes are inherent and regarded as talents. If their attempts at accomplishing a task are unsuccessful, it is commonly ascribed to a deficiency in aptitude and talent. Individuals who fall under the Growth Mindset category, conversely, harbor a steadfast belief that through proper dedication, any endeavor can be accomplished. Adopting such a mentality not only alleviates stress but also fosters a greater level of achievement.

Methodology 3: Employing Timeline Therapy as an Intervention for Depression

In a state of depression, individuals tend to gravitate towards past experiences more prominently. It is an inherent component of the inherent depressive cycle. Due to the presence of depression, you will perceive the world as immutable, thus lacking the ability to exert an influential impact on its potential transformation, regardless of your actions.

Depression impairs one's ability to recognize the possibility of positive experiences in the world, resulting in a withdrawal from loved ones due to a perceived inability to provide uplifting experiences.

Visualization of the Human Body Field

It is imperative to acknowledge the existence of an electromagnetic field that envelops your physical being, whether or not you are conscious of its presence. As the exchange of energy takes place between the brain and the nervous system, the generation of this magnetic field occurs. Furthermore, all neurological pathways within your anatomical system contribute to the intricate electromagnetic field enveloping your physique. Similar to the examination of one's cardiac function at a medical facility, the observation pertains to the scrutiny of the electromagnetic field enveloping the heart.

Each individual culture will perceive the human body in their own distinct manner. The origins of this perspective can be traced back to the way it was perceived in civilizations of antiquity.

Certain Native American cultures in the Southeast employed the depiction of waves in their artwork as a means to portray the electromagnetic field that the human body inherently generates, as this frequency is an inherent part of our natural ecosystem. They recognized the inherent connection and mutual reliance between the physical form and the natural surroundings.

Throughout the annals of civilization, various societies have denoted the magnetic field as an aura, a concept that can be traced back to the very nascent stages of human development. Numerous auras are perceived as vibrant color halos emanating from an individual's head. However, upon examining the cultural practices of Egypt, one would observe that the aura envelops the entirety of an individual's physical form.

In China, it was believed that the energetic force surrounding individuals, often referred to as an aura or magnetic field, embodied the concept of Chi. Similarly, in India, this force is known as prana. However, within the Hindu culture, it was believed that the magnetic field was reserved for those who had attained complete enlightenment.

When engaging in the visualization of the magnetic field surrounding your body, it is advisable to conceive of it as a spherical entity that envelops your body from all directions, essentially encasing you within a sphere. Given that nerves are present throughout various regions of your body, the electromagnetic field will propagate across your body, transitioning from one nerve to another.

All objects within your field of vision shall be deemed as encompassing your active awareness. This consciousness is dynamic as it grants you the ability to perceive it and anticipate forthcoming events. When operating a vehicle, one is capable of observing all elements ahead, thus requiring focused attention on the road ahead due to clear visibility. Furthermore, it should be noted that the entire landscape before you is susceptible to alteration, ultimately shaping the course of your future.

Conversely, any content that lies in your past is regarded as dormant consciousness. This is due to the fact that it is no longer visible. Regard it as your previous experiences. One's ability to perceive their past is presently non-existent, and accordingly, any attempts to modify it are rendered ineffectual, thus rendering it devoid of influence in one's life. Indeed, you will inevitably confront the consequences of the errors committed in your past, yet regrettably, there remains no viable course of action to rectify them, as they are now firmly situated in your history.

As previously elucidated, the subject at hand encompasses the trajectory of our existence and the prevailing circumstances of our present reality. Consider it from the perspective of working towards an objective. You will diligently undertake all requisite procedures to ensure the successful attainment of the desired objective. As long as we devote thought to it, it will continue to hold significance in our lives. However, once we cease striving for or have attained the objective, our subconscious will relegate it to our past. Given that we have ceased contemplation of it, it immediately assumes a dormant role in our lives. Consequently, when we reflect upon something that we have previously overcome, it inevitably recaptures our attention and necessitates our active involvement until we are able to relegate it to the past and relinquish its hold on us once more.

An instance of proactive consciousness can be observed when an individual strives to obtain a higher position within their professional setting. To obtain the promotion, you will need to successfully navigate a series of strategic actions that will serve to facilitate your ascension to that esteemed position. Whether comprehension is attained or not, the outcome is not necessarily subject to personal volition, yet it remains an aspiration to be pursued. Provided you maintain your focus on a particular matter, it will remain within your conscious awareness.

One illustration of passive comprehension can be found in the disagreement you had with your spouse. Although it may require some time to expunge the hurtful remarks uttered during the argument, you will eventually overcome the negative impact and relegate them to insignificance. Upon successful completion of that particular step, your cognitive faculties will facilitate its relegation to the past, allowing abstention from its contemplation. Although it may resurface in your consciousness upon encountering them again in a conflict, it will remain dormant until that particular juncture.

Given that individuals experiencing depression tend to have a propensity to concentrate on negative aspects, it is more likely that their attention will be directed towards inactive matters, predominantly because the adverse encounters in their life are also lodged within the inactive regions of their brain. Similar to the previous scenario where you engaged in a conflict with your spouse, the hurtful remarks shared during that altercation will likely remain etched in your memory, exacerbating the sense that the disagreement has not reached resolution.

Although this assertion is entirely unfounded, the presence of depression hampers one's ability to disengage from the negative encounter. The statements that were uttered will persistently resonate in your mind, thus rendering your apparent mental inactivity as active due to the recurrent retrieval and contemplation of these thoughts.

Assumption 1: The representation or depiction of something, such as a map, should not be mistaken for the actual physical reality or experience.

The meaning:

Envision a scenario where the weather in Scotland is splendidly sunny. As you may be aware, Scotland is characterized by a predominantly cold climate. According to a resident of Scottish descent residing in the area, the climatic conditions can be described as pleasant when there is ample sunshine. An Australian resident in Scotland describes the climate as chilly. Additionally, as you may be aware, what may appear as a sunny day in Scotland may still be perceived as cold to an individual from Australia, where the climate is predominantly hot.

Envision a scenario in which the Scottish gentleman and the Australian individual convene and engage in a conversation and intellectual exchange pertaining to meteorological conditions. The Scotsman provides evidence of warm weather, while the Australians provide evidence of cold weather. Each individual endeavors to substantiate their PERSPECTIVE. This implies that each individual endeavors to persuade the other with their own perspectives.

Whose viewpoint do you believe to be accurate? The response is that both options are accurate. Every individual expresses the truth based on their own unique perspective.

Perhaps you perceive the ongoing debate between the Scotsman and the Australian as frivolous; however, allow me to inform you that there exists a considerable number of individuals engaging in such exchanges, articulating viewpoints and offering arguments on a myriad of subjects.

Have you ever engaged in a constructive dialogue with a friend or family member with the intention of enhancing a certain aspect of their life, only to find yourselves embroiled in conflict instead? Probably yes. I am aware that you hold the belief that the individual with whom you engage in heated discussions lacks intelligence. Regrettably, it is likely that he also perceives this unfavorable situation.

The positive aspect is that your statement is accurate, while the negative aspect is that his statement is likewise accurate. Both of you hold valid viewpoints based on your respective perspectives. You possess the same attributes as the Scotsman and the Australian, both of whom are correct in their respective perspectives.

The reality may not align with your perceptions, but it must be acknowledged that these lines are being read by you, thus constituting the truth. In reality, you are either focused or unfocused. It is a fact that you are currently conscious...

Human individuals have the capacity to internally construct personal and subjective realities in order to depict and interpret the world they inhabit. As a result, individuals react and respond to their internalized experiences rather than the objective reality that exists within them.

A considerable number of individuals tend to react to their own perceptions rather than the objective reality presented to them. Two individuals may observe the same occurrence; however, their reactions to it can diverge significantly. This is attributable to our limited access to an objective depiction of reality, resulting in our insufficient understanding thereof. Our perception of reality is shaped by our sensory perceptions, our cognitive frameworks, and our individual perspectives, or more precisely, our personal conceptualization of reality that inherently carries underlying motivations. Fortunately, NLP has the ability to transform the ineffective "maps" you possess into something valuable, thereby enhancing your life. One can enhance their understanding by incorporating additional data and exploring diverse interpretations, thereby broadening their perspective through the establishment of fresh analogies.

The issue with our comprehension lies in our unawareness of our own ignorance. Have you ever encountered an individual who feigns omniscience and presents themselves as the epitome of intellectual prowess? Presumably, we have all encountered individuals who take delight in providing exhaustive explanations and positioning themselves as the most intelligent.

The representation of reality provided by a map serves as a reminder of our limited understanding, highlighting the existence of unknown unknowns. In a similar vein, when we refer to our physical map, it provides a depiction of the terrain's appearance, but it remains distinct from the actual territory.

The recommended course of action for you to undertake:

To cultivate this presupposition, there are several measures that one ought to undertake. Primarily, it is imperative to exercise humility and guard against allowing one's ego to dictate, dispelling any notion of possessing comprehensive knowledge.

It would be wise for you to recognize that your knowledge is not devoid of limitations; you hold the belief that your understanding is all-encompassing and expect others to heed your opinions. Your ego is the driving force behind such beliefs. On occasion, individuals may encounter a predicament and believe they have exhausted all possible solutions, whereas in truth, they have not explored every avenue due to the influence of their ego.

Make an effort to acquire extensive knowledge, as you possess limited understanding and are unaware of the extent of your lack of knowledge. Inculcating a regular practice of learning will impart the realization that our knowledge is inherently limited within the realm of existence.

Once you become cognizant of your limited knowledge, it is imperative to exhibit respect towards alternative perspectives. I understand that there may be instances when encountering someone's opinion may strike you as unintelligent; however, before engaging in discussion and debate with that individual, it is imperative to empathize with their perspective by putting yourself in their position, contemplating with their cognition, and perceiving through their lens. Refrain from using derogatory terms such as 'stupid' or 'ignorant' in any context, including your thoughts, as these labels correspond to his perception of matters. And even if one believes that their opinion is true, it is inevitable that others may perceive it as foolish. Therefore, it is imperative to cultivate a deep sense of respect for differing viewpoints.

The advantages that you will obtain:

When one truly comprehends the fact that the map does not represent the territory, one gains the understanding that their beliefs, knowledge, and opinions may be inaccurate, just as there are many individuals who possess erroneous understandings. Thus, you are renouncing your preconceived notions and committing to impartiality.

Your ego will not be excessively inflated, and as you are likely aware, your inflated ego will not contribute to your personal advancement. Please keep in mind that your ego should not be regarded as your friend.

Individuals with an inflated sense of self will find themselves obstructed and constrained in their perspectives. Should these perspectives consist of negative or detrimental qualities, it is probable that their lives will reflect the same negativity and toxicity. And it is essential to keep in mind that one may possess erroneous convictions and remain unaware of them, as one's own beliefs lack the capacity to reveal such inaccuracies.

If one occasionally entertains thoughts as to the reasons behind a negative existence, it would be prudent to acknowledge that one's beliefs may be the root cause. If one contemplates as to why their life tends to exhibit negativity, it could possibly be inferred that their beliefs adopt a pessimistic standpoint.

Given your strong faith in your own beliefs and the respect you hold for them, I kindly urge you to extend that same respect towards the beliefs held by others. It is important to be aware that individuals typically find it unfavorable when their viewpoints are contradicted. It appears that you may prefer to avoid encountering differing viewpoints.

Individuals who possess an inclination towards embracing novel beliefs and perspectives tend to excel as problem solvers. This predisposition empowers them to explore innovative solutions across various domains, thereby transcending the limitations of a fixed mindset. Rather than feigning omniscience, such individuals consistently display a thirst for knowledge, consistently updating their mental frameworks in pursuit of an enhanced quality of life.

The advantages you will receive:

Once you come to acknowledge that you are not inherently flawed, but rather whole and complete, you will cultivate an attitude of gratitude, consequently augmenting the level of contentment and overall joy you experience throughout your life. Moreover, this will propel you towards progress rather than fostering a disposition of complaint and victimhood.

Another trait that one must possess is a modest and humble disposition, as allowing one's ego to dominate can ultimately undermine one's own sense of contentment. Perhaps your ego occasionally provides you with a temporary sense of satisfaction, but in the long run, it is not sustainable. Over time, your ego will result in feelings of despair and emotional unrest.

Furthermore, an additional valuable advantage that will be conferred upon you is the enhanced insight and self-awareness resulting from perceiving things with utmost clarity within your mental faculties. In addition, you will develop a stronger comprehension of others, consequently yielding additional advantages and an increased ability to discern when to seek assistance. One will discern the true extent of their anguish and necessity for assistance, distinguishing it from merely bemoaning a trivial predicament and catastrophizing its consequences.

Assumption 11: Every Individual Possesses the Necessary Means

"The most significant constraint on an individual lies not in the pursuits they desire but are unable to achieve, but rather in the endeavors they haven't contemplated undertaking." - Richard Bandler-

The meaning:

Are you experiencing a sense of stagnation or impediment in your journey? Maybe you were. Likely, you perceived yourself as having limited alternatives and inadequate means to address the issue at hand. Indeed, in reality, you possess the necessary resources both in the past and at present.

The issue at hand arises when one adopts the restrictive belief that they possess neither resources nor options, rendering them devoid of any possibilities or alternatives.

Throughout history, mankind has perennially possessed the necessary means to fulfill their needs, yet oftentimes individuals fail to recognize these resources due to the constraining perspective of perceived scarcity.

By taking a moment to ponder and formulate an appropriate inquiry pertaining to your problem-solving endeavor or objective, you shall uncover the necessary resources.

The recommended course of action:

It is imperative to consistently seek inquiries regarding potential solutions, strategies for achieving desired objectives, and the most optimal approaches to particular situations. It is crucial not to passively respond to circumstances without taking any action. Instead, take proactive measures to actively address and overcome challenges in order to attain desired outcomes.

Remain receptive to all potential alternatives that may be available to you. Do not hesitate to explore novel experiences. Proceed with the task regardless and approach it with a positive outlook regarding the ultimate result.

The advantages you will receive:

You will possess resources only if you maintain the belief that you possess them. This is a matter of significance as it pertains to the lack of resources, which is when one holds the belief that.

Recognizing the availability of resources enables one to continually accrue additional provisions.

Another advantage is that you will possess exceptional problem-solving abilities, owing to your adeptness in leveraging available resources and taking decisive action. Additionally, you will acquire the knowledge of effectively attaining your goals in life by utilizing the available resources at your disposal.

The manifestation of representative systems in eye movements.

According to the findings of John Grinder and Richard Bandler, pioneers of NLP, it has been determined that the ocular movements exhibited by individuals are directly correlated to their brain's information processing methods, namely visual, auditory, or kinesthetic.

When one recollects visual images, there is a subsequent upward and rightward movement of the pupils. When engaging in mental imagery, such as attempting to envision something we have not yet observed, it is typical for our pupils to shift upwards and towards the left.

When we engage in reflection, understanding, or perception of visual stimuli, our gaze is typically directed straight ahead or towards the upward direction.

Upon recollecting sounds and words, our pupils undergo a lateral shift towards the right. When engaging in cognitive processes such as the mental generation of thoughts, verbal expression, textual composition, or the creation of melodies, our pupils demonstrate a horizontal leftward movement.

When engaged in auditory perception or introspection, the pupils exhibit a leftward and downward movement.

When experiencing heightened sensations and receiving kinesthetic signals, it is commonly observed that the pupils tend to exhibit a downward vertical or downward right movement.

It is important to take into consideration that this scheme applies exclusively to individuals who are right-handed - whereas for left-handed individuals, the direction of the pupils' movements will be reversed in each instance.

Undoubtedly, these movements are typically minimal, yet they remain detectable in the majority of instances. Exceptions may arise in situations where an individual is overwhelmed by a multitude of images simultaneously or experiences a state of confusion, rendering them unable to maintain focus. In this particular scenario, it is possible that his pupils could exhibit a state of immobility or demonstrate erratic movement. However, it is frequently observed that there is a strong correlation between the primary governing structure and the actions undertaken by the students. One can be persuaded of its validity by observing the experiences of others.

Practical task

Recall the appearance of your beloved childhood toy and, as you engage in this recollection, take heed of the motion of your gaze. If one is predominantly right-handed, it is highly probable that the instinctive response would involve automatically veering towards the right and upwards. The ocular orientation exhibited is indicative of an individual who recollects visual stimuli.

Envision, if you will, the semblance of an object that eludes your possession, yet exists solely within the realm of your aspirations—a dwelling, a luxurious garment, an automobile, or any other desired entity. Envision the hue, form, and incorporate various elements. Monitor the gaze direction. Observe the eye movements. Keep tabs on the eye position. Track the line of sight. Follow the trajectory of the eyes. It is highly probable that the pupils made a leftward and upward turn. This is a distinguishing motion observed when attempting to formulate a mental depiction within the realm of our imagination.

Direct your focus towards your body and assess the areas where muscle tension is present. Please verify the exact placement of the eyes. During the process of scanning kinesthetic images, it is observed that the pupils exhibit an automatic movement towards the right and downward direction.

Recall your preferred musical composition and observe the direction of the pupils during the process of reminiscing. Right horizontally? This phenomenon occurs when we recollect words and, more broadly, any auditory stimuli.

Examine your emotions and provide a response to your own query. Follow the pupils. They proceed laterally towards the left while we partake in introspective contemplation and attentively perceive our own thoughts.

In that case, proceed with your customary operations. Do not consciously fixate your gaze - allow your eyes to move naturally, as is customary. However, assign yourself the obligation to periodically observe the posture of your students. Undoubtedly, it will come to your attention that your eyes exhibit a particular inclination towards a certain position, one that is more frequently observed than others. However, there exist certain provisions that are less frequently encountered, with a few being exceptionally scarce. In this manner, you will ascertain the predominant functioning mode of your brain, as well as identify the modes that are employed infrequently or perhaps scarcely at all.

Please categorize your areas of proficiency and areas needing improvement.

Having determined your primary representative system, you can now obtain a comprehensive understanding of your strengths and weaknesses. Indeed, representative systems are viable. However, even in the event of training all three systems, one will inevitably retain its predominant role.

This indicates that even amidst challenging and taxing circumstances, it will retain utmost priority. It is crucial to understand that the timely execution of appropriate and accurate actions holds utmost significance.

Consider a scenario in which one must undertake a task at a designated moment. For instance, let us contemplate the act of deactivating the kitchen oven. For individuals who possess a preference for visual stimuli, a written note or image serves as the most effective means of reminder, preferably one that is vivid and easily noticeable. Alternatively, those inclined towards auditory stimulation benefit from the use of an alarm clock. As for individuals who respond well to physical sensations, any bodily signal can serve as a reminder, although it is advised to avoid relying on the presence of undesirable odors such as burnt food. Instead, utilizing a timer to activate a heater or air conditioning unit, whose subsequent shutdown can then serve as a signal to turn off the oven, is recommended.

Furthermore, possessing a comprehensive understanding of your primary systems will enable you to make informed decisions regarding the most effective strategies to achieve the desired outcomes. In order to accomplish this, it is imperative to possess an understanding of both your areas of proficiency and limitations.

What types of actions can individuals with visual, audio, and kinesthetic inclinations effectively perform, and what attributes do they lack, giving rise to their inherent "limitations"?

Strengths of visual individuals. They are adept at swiftly navigating in all types of surroundings. They possess the ability to rapidly perceive and analyze information. They will outperform their peers in domains requiring prompt decision-making. Furthermore, visuals demonstrate exceptional capabilities in the realm of strategic planning. They possess the capacity to envision the tangible outcome of forthcoming endeavors.

By virtue of their ability to visualize their aspirations, they possess a clear understanding of their desires.

Weaknesses of visual individuals. They place excessive reliance on visual stimuli, but it is important to recognize that not everything that catches the eye is of high value. By solely depending on external appearances, they run the risk of misjudging individuals and obtaining aesthetically pleasing yet subpar or superfluous possessions. They possess a limited capacity to sustain their focus on a single activity for an extended duration, as they have a tendency to quickly lose interest and become disengaged. This can be attributed to the continuous fluctuation and diversion of their attention caused by the ever-changing "pictures" presented by the external environment.

Strengths of audio individuals. They possess the ability to actively listen and comprehensively comprehend the perspectives of others. Based on nuanced inflections and variations in speech, one can construct a rather comprehensive portrayal of an individual, encompassing their emotions, thoughts, and intentions. It is exceedingly arduous to mislead them; indeed, they possess the capacity to perceive not merely the literal words spoken, but also the underlying implications. They possess the ability to establish a shared means of communication with nearly everyone, showcasing their mastery in the realm of interpersonal interactions. They engage in dialogue not just with individuals, but with the entirety of the world surrounding them, as they perceive the entire world as resonating and expressive. Possessing a comprehensive grasp of the universal language, they effortlessly achieve a state of harmony, exhibiting the ability to concur with individuals and concepts in a literal sense, regardless of their nature.

Weaknesses of audio individuals. They are unable to swiftly familiarize themselves with their surroundings. They require adequate time for contemplation, consideration of diverse perspectives, and introspection. Consequently, engaging in activities necessitating prompt decision-making is inadvisable for them. They can rapidly become fatigued by the overwhelming abundance of visual stimuli. They are also not recommended to spend an extended period of time in noisy environments.

Strengths of kinesthetic individuals. They experience a heightened state of presence in their surroundings, enabling them to derive pleasure from it, as they possess a profound sense of vitality and an ongoing connection with the true nature of reality. By their inherent disposition, they are individuals who engage in practical application, experimentation, and subject everything to personal sensory scrutiny. They prove challenging to manipulate as they place greater reliance on their own intuitive observations compared to the words of others. They possess a keen aptitude for comprehending body language, and through analyzing facial expressions, gestures, and movements, they are capable of ascertaining the veracity about an individual, notwithstanding their ardent attempts at concealing it.

Weaknesses of kinesthetic individuals. They encounter challenges when transitioning between different types of activities. It proves to be challenging in occupations where agility is necessitated. They may become entrenched in their experiences, given the prolonged duration required for transitioning from one sensation to another. For every endeavor, they require a setting characterized by a greater degree of tranquility in comparison to that which is preferred by the general populace. Enduring physical discomfort poses a considerable challenge. Haste and stress are to be avoided in their case. It requires a longer duration for relaxation, preferably in a passive manner.

If the prominent shortcomings of your primary representative system are conspicuously evident within your personal abilities, deliberately involving yourself in the cultivation of alternative representative systems may prove advantageous. As a result of this, you will cultivate a more harmonious and well-rounded character. Furthermore, it is important to note that such training will undoubtedly broaden your understanding of the world, shield you from narrow perspectives, enable you to obtain maximum information from all sources, regardless of the circumstances. Ultimately, this will considerably enhance your chances of succeeding in any given situation.

Principles Of Interpreting Human Behavior

The prowess of discerning and swiftly comprehending individuals is a paramount asset in comprehending human nature and assisting them in managing their internal experiences and sentiments. Individuals with the ability to discern the inner emotions of others possess exceptional talent and have the capacity to achieve remarkable outcomes. It will aid individuals in enhancing their interpersonal connections, professional achievements, and social aptitude.

In order to examine human behavior comprehensively, it is essential to delve into various facets that exert a direct or indirect influence on individuals, encompassing their values, lifestyle, cognitive processes, and belief systems. Behavior analysts typically conduct analyses on individuals experiencing behavioral challenges, in order to investigate the impact of environmental influences on their behavior.

Examining individuals' conduct leads to a profound comprehension of their character, assuming that one is equipped with ample psychological knowledge. When endeavoring to examine human behavior, it is imperative to analyze the entirety of the details rather than isolating individual components for analysis. In the event that an individual exhibits a fear or apprehension towards cats, it would be prudent not to presume that their feelings are solely attributed to a prior negative encounter with felines. It is imperative to consider all potential facets of her life that may have precipitated the development of this apprehension. Perhaps the apprehension towards cats might have been triggered by their aversion.

Communication has perpetually served as a vital aspect in the realm of human interaction. Moreover, it has been asserted by experts that communication primarily relies on non-verbal cues. The individual is likely to fail to grasp the message in the absence of adequate internal and external resources employed for interpreting body language. Therefore, it is imperative to prioritize the skill of interpreting individuals during the communication process.

To gain a comprehensive grasp of this book and effectively harness your capacity to influence others, it is imperative that you acquire the skill of discerning individuals' thoughts and emotions by attentively interpreting both their spoken and unspoken cues, while also recognizing their underlying motivations or Secondary Gain. Upon recognizing this as an external resource leveraging your internal capabilities, you will be better equipped to attain your desired results. It is essential to bear in mind that gaining an understanding of the patterns of human behavior and acquiring the ability to decipher body language enables one to perceive beyond the superficial mask that most individuals present. Hidden beneath the facade of an individual's flawless smile lies a certain element of sorrow, and by employing the principles elucidated within this literary work, one can discern the true essence of individuals beyond their self-presentation. In addition, through the utilization of the fundamental principles of neuro-linguistic programming, one can more accurately assess the complete dynamics of interpersonal communication, without being misdirected by social conventions that are perceived merely as courteous gestures.

To comprehend individuals, one must possess the ability to discern their genuine emotions, primarily by paying less heed to their explicit expressions. This stems from the understanding that deception is an inherent characteristic prevalent among all individuals. Hence, verbal communication does not provide an assurance of veracity. In the absence of veracity, discerning individuals becomes a futile endeavor. The purpose of reading people is to gather insights into the reality. It is imperative to ascertain their genuine perspectives, underlying thoughts, and emotional responses pertaining to a given scenario. Having knowledge of the truth would facilitate your comprehension of that individual's character, thereby enabling you to interact with them adeptly and exert influence over them.

Moreover, it is crucial to bear in mind that the ability to accurately assess individuals becomes unattainable when one remains fixated on past grievances or holds onto subjective biases. It is imperative that you relinquish any preconceived notions and biases towards individuals in order to accurately interpret body language, as such biases can significantly skew one's perception of reality. Consequently, you may develop erroneous presumptions about an individual, thereby compromising the entirety of your manipulative endeavor. In order to exert an influence over the actions of others, it is imperative to possess an understanding of their genuine inclinations. In order to achieve this, it is necessary to acquire an understanding of human behavioral patterns and the intricacies of nonverbal communication.

To comprehend the contents of another individual's gaze

If the notion holds true that the eyes serve as conduits to one's innermost self, then it becomes imperative to contemplate this aspect when endeavoring to employ NLP techniques upon another individual. In order to initiate the examination of someone's eye movements, it is imperative to pose a sequence of inquiries and carefully observe the trajectory of their gaze while they respond. Initiate the conversation by inquiring about a matter of fact, specifically one that you are certain the individual will respond to with honesty. One could inquire about the individual's name or solicit information regarding the date of their birth. Take careful note of their gaze. This enables you to ascertain the true course they are taking in their statements. Subsequently, in the event that they deviate from the original course, it is highly probable that they will be disseminating falsehoods.

Lastly, it is advisable to inquire about a matter with the intention of eliciting an untruthful response from the individual in question. Therefore, if you are aware of the individual's underlying insecurity regarding their salary, inquire tactfully whether their income approximates a slightly higher range than you are confident it actually does. There is a significant probability that they will concur with you given their reluctance to disclose the lesser sum that they perceive as a vulnerability. Observing the ocular behavior and vocal inflection of an individual will aid in discerning potential falsehoods they may present in the future.

Technique #1 for Psychological Influence: Unauthorized Implementation of Hypnosis

Numerous individuals presently resort to mesmerism as a means to aid in the retrieval of cherished memories and even past existences. In certain instances, individuals resort to a state of trance in order to facilitate the modification of something significant to them.

There is nothing inappropriate about seeking elective treatment. Indeed, numerous individuals have proclaimed the potential groundbreaking nature of sleep-inducing meetings.

Regardless, the danger lies in entrusting yourself to a trance specialist of whom you have minimal knowledge. You may unwittingly be endangering your well-being and financial stability.

When faced with someone claiming to possess the ability to mesmerize you, refrain from allowing them to experiment on you, even if you harbor doubts regarding the potency of the phenomenon known as hypnosis. In any case, it is advisable for you to be accompanied by an individual whom you have faith in.

Psychological Influence Method #2: Imposing Isolation from Familiar Surroundings

One of the more malignant cognitive programming methods is that of disassociation. This represents the juncture at which you find yourself effectively severed from your family, associates, and all that is familiar.

It is plausible that you may not regard it as a matter of great importance; nevertheless, experiencing detachment from all others can significantly impact one's mental state. Social separation not just strips you of your own convictions, it likewise shapes you into whatever the individual or a gathering of individuals need you to think.

In the absence of any supporting individuals, you would be compelled to select the option that aligns with the prevailing perspective. In order to refrain from being mentally conditioned in such a manner, it is advisable to remain vigilant towards individuals who insist on influencing you away from your loved ones.

Technique #3: Employment of Fear-Based Methods that Exploit Cognitive Processes

Alarm strategies can encompass a wide range of factors, ranging from potential hazards to discreet cognitive challenges. This act of brain manipulation exploits an individual's fear and undoubtedly ranks among the most perilous endeavors.

At the point when you feel undermined in any capacity, it's significant that you look for the assistance of your companions, family and the correct specialists. The presence of neurosis can lead to the realization of actions that would not typically be undertaken under normal circumstances.

These cognitive manipulation techniques exhibit an almost imperceptible nature. In any case, by exercising heightened awareness and seeking appropriate assistance, you can now effectively shield yourself against individuals who employ deceptive tactics, thus ensuring your personal safety.

Utilizing Optimistic Mental Imagery For Extraordinary Achievement

To achieve remarkable transformations in your life, overall wellness, drive, and perspective, it is essential to sincerely embrace and practice the technique of positive visualization.

You may be acquainted with the concept of positive visualization in sports, wherein athletes and sports enthusiasts employ their imaginative abilities to unlock their utmost capabilities. Rest assured, you too can harness this technique without the necessity of pursuing any specialized training program.

Visualization is an inherently powerful methodology for achieving success given its routine incorporation in our daily lives.

Please allocate a brief period of time to contemplate your agenda for the upcoming week. May I inquire about your plans for the remainder of the day or possibly tomorrow? What activities do you have planned for the upcoming weekend?

When these factors are brought to the forefront of your thoughts, the skill of visualization is being exercised. You are employing your cognitive faculties to construct a mental representation of the forthcoming event, akin to perusing a literary work, which, in turn, instills a sense of acquaintance with said event, notwithstanding one's lack of experiential involvement.

Furthermore, the manner in which you perceive said event will inevitably influence both your subjective encounter and, in all likelihood, its ultimate result as well.

Suppose that you have a scheduled dental appointment tomorrow. Typically, individuals tend to have an aversion towards dental appointments, much like the general population. If you engage in excessive concern and construct a distressing and menacing mental representation of the upcoming appointment, it is probable that you will experience heightened fear and apprehension on the scheduled day. Your body and mind will have already automated their response to be cautious of the impending danger. Conversely, in the event that the event had not been thoroughly contemplated, it is probable that a reduced level of anxiety would be experienced during the occurrence.

We have the capacity to leverage the potential of visualization and employ it in a constructive manner to enhance our motivation, counteract depression, transcend self-esteem challenges, and ultimately fulfill our objectives.

Visualizing can bear resemblance to experiencing dreams in three dimensions. However, visualization encompasses more than mere daydreaming; it entails perceiving the path towards accomplishing one's objective.

Our next step entails employing visualization techniques to effectively apply them to the S.M.A.R.T goals that you have already delineated.

Kindly attempt the provided exercise:

1) Relax, gently shut your eyes, and select one of the goals you have previously established.

2) Employ mental imagery to envision the requisite actions for attaining your

objectives, visualizing yourself effectively executing each step and triumphing. It is imperative to envision a mental representation of yourself progressing methodically through the entirety of the expedition, triumphing over any obstacles encountered.

Observing oneself achieving success at each individual stage will engender the requisite motivation to foster the courage required to pursue one's aspirations. Additionally, it will redirect your attention towards strategizing solutions for challenges and barriers, enhancing your subliminal conviction in your ability to manifest any imagined outcome into tangible existence.

3) Commence the process of visualizing this specific objective, constructing a

vivid mental representation of its realization with utmost precision. How would it appear? What sensations would one experience? What would be your internal emotional state? Grant yourself the freedom to indulge in your imagination and explore the possibilities it presents in practical terms.

4) Now that you have enhanced the clarity of your vision to the fullest extent possible, employ all of your senses. Enhance the brightness, enlarge the size, and bring it nearer. Enable your mind to embody your accomplishment.

Take note of your emotions and consciously permit them to manifest within your physical being.

5) Gradually and delicately open your eyes and bring your awareness back to

the present moment. You may experience the sensation of having indulged in a brief period of slumber. Rest assured, this is completely typical.

Positive visualization can also serve as a highly effective strategy during trying periods that you encounter in your life. Suppose you encounter a setback along your journey towards your objective, in such instances, employing positive visualization can assist in perceiving the obstacle merely as a temporary hurdle, enabling you to persistently advance towards a more promising future.

By employing the technique of visualizing yourself successfully reaching a goal and cultivating the sensation of already living that achievement prior to its actualization, you enhance your subconscious stimulation and prime your conscious mind to discern feasible strategies for surmounting these hindrances.

If one is able to conceptualize each sequential process required in order to attain a specific objective, the subsequent task merely entails the efficient execution of the anticipated steps.

Nowadays, there may be instances where individuals are hesitant to engage in the mental process of envisioning overcoming a challenge, due to the presence of a combination of emotions such as anxiety, fears, and self-doubt.

Allow us to proceed with the subsequent chapter, wherein we shall acquire the knowledge to deliberately evoke various emotions through the utilization of anchoring techniques.

Do you desire serenity amidst tumultuous circumstances? Do you desire a sense of tranquility prior to an event that typically induces high levels of anxiety? Anchoring is the answer.

Applications Of Nlp

Visual Squash

This is a method employed in the field of NLP that facilitates the recognition of each component as a means to reconstruct a cohesive entity. Using this methodology, every component is seamlessly incorporated to a significantly enhanced degree in comparison to the previous constraints, thereby attaining a state of harmonious integration and entirety. Every individual component is delineated and categorized based on its specific role and consequential impact on other elements within the system. This method is employed to address the discord among various components, ensuring a stable work environment conducive to systematic completion of tasks.

The notion of visual squash was exclusively stumbled upon in order to facilitate the reconditioning of prior thoughts or emotions into a more optimistic state. It is crucial for an individual to acquire the skills of deconditioning, which refers to the removal of the pre-existing mindset or beliefs that may impose limitations or impede their progress. This process is then complemented by reconditioning, which involves replacing the outdated perspective with a new and advantageous one. Individuals can promptly transform negative thoughts and emotions into positive ones once they acquire the knowledge and skills surrounding the principles of deconditioning and reconditioning.

"The procedure of visual compression encompasses:

a) Observe the adverse pattern: This entails suppressing the mental image obtained from the visual observation. It is imperative to consider the adverse implications of the idea and convey them through a vivid portrayal. For instance, if one does not assume a leadership role, it is important to carefully consider the potential ramifications. Not assuming a leadership position may lead to minimal attendance at social gatherings, and could result in a deterioration of one's standing within their social circle. Amplify in order to emphasize the unfavorable concept.

b) Envisioning the substitution pattern: Subsequently, upon harboring the negative notion of not being the leader, you can counteract it by cultivating a positive thought through cultivating a diametrically opposite mental image. Rather than perceiving yourself as lacking leadership qualities, affirm yourself as an exceptional leader, unrivaled by any other. Generate vivid mental imagery wherein individuals dutifully adhere to your directives and exhibit a profound affinity towards your authoritative instructions. Feel free to embellish the situation according to your preferences.

c) Connect the two states: It is necessary to establish a connection between the initial negative thought and the subsequent positive thought. It is now entirely up to you to select the suitable scenario that will establish the connection between the two states. Envision and conceive your own narrative depicting how the initial uncomfortable situation or scenario may culminate in a positive outcome. Exhibit creative thinking through the utilization of your personal imagination.

d) Unlearn and Dismiss: This entails the deliberate process of eliminating all detrimental thoughts from one's consciousness, focusing solely on retaining a final thread of affirmative thinking. One can employ the power of mental imagery to envision the act of discarding a voluminous quantity of dust from one's hand, thereby fostering the refurbishment of their own viewpoint.

e) Rehabilitation: When shifting towards a more optimistic viewpoint, you will discover that your transformed mentality and demeanor yield advantageous outcomes for your personal growth. You will gain proficiency in effective communication and possess the capacity to provide leadership to others. Upon attaining this accomplishment, should you happen to entertain any lingering pessimistic thoughts, your cognitive faculties will promptly associate them with your revitalized state of optimism, as a matter of course.

Collapsing Anchor

This strategy typically involves manipulating the anchors that are established through state linkage. In order to sustain a favorable perspective on life, individuals must acquire the skill of detaching themselves from negative influences. The anchor or trigger effectively elicits the desired mental state that one intends to cultivate during the pursuit of a specific goal. Nevertheless, the presence of negative anchors promptly induces a state of bewilderment and skepticism, prompting individuals to feel uncertain or doubtful if these anchors have been initially linked to an unfavorable encounter. It is imperative that you possess the knowledge and skills required to disengage these anchors, thereby disassociating them from their associated negative thoughts and emotions. The sequential procedure for the collapsing of anchors is as follows:

a) Identify the anchor : The anchor can be anything like thought, feeling, disability or experience. There may exist multiple anchors, however, one must systematically discern and progressively eliminate the negative anchors in order to effectively dismantle them. Once the anchor has been identified, commence efforts towards its resolution. An instance of this would be having the anchor of anger and a tendency towards short temper.

b) Select the alternative: In order to select the alternative, it is necessary to identify a positive stimulus that can substitute your negative reference point.

This can be achieved by selecting a completely contrasting reference point. To illustrate, during our discussion on anger, the term "joy" can be employed as an instance. Joy can manifest itself through various facets, such as the experience of being cherished or the appreciation of comedic elements. Envision the alternative that aligns most closely with your emotional requirements.

c) Establish a connection between the alternative options: After making a choice among the alternatives, proceed to determine the corresponding emotion. For instance, if joy is the emotion you have selected, you can consider recalling joyful moments as a means of invoking that alternative, such as engaging in quality time with cherished individuals or engaging in playful activities with your beloved pet. One can enhance their resourcefulness by bringing a physical representation such as a photograph capturing the presence of their loved ones. Every time you reminisce about the pleasant moments or gaze upon the image, a surge of happiness will effortlessly envelop you.

d) Disable the anchor: When dealing with an external anchor, it can be effortlessly substituted with an external, well-endowed state. To accomplish this, merely eliminate the detrimental correlation and substitute it with a fresh external reference point that facilitates the cultivation of a positive demeanor. If the anchor is a in eternal memory like any traumatic experience, then link it with a positive experience and store it in your mind. Whenever you contemplate upon the traumatic event, employ the technique of mentally conjuring an alternative internal memory as a means to weaken and ultimately supersede the negative one.

Application: Following this comprehensive process, you will now possess the ability to overcome negative thoughts by embracing positive alternatives. These alternatives should evoke heightened and more poignant emotions than the negative patterns, ensuring that you can fully detach from the associated triggers. Utilize this knowledge in practical scenarios to assess and ascertain the extent of practice and visualization required. Subsequently, you will be equipped to demonstrate a favorable disposition towards life.

f) Cognitive restructuring: It has been asserted that "not all behavior exhibits perfection." It signifies that while certain things may be well-intentioned, they may also possess negative attributes or elements. The majority of individuals do not subscribe to the notion that unfavorable circumstances can coexist with the most honorable intentions. Every behavior possesses underlying positive motives, but the pursuit of these intentions may encounter imperfections that manifest in a negative manner. The concept of positive intent entails acknowledging and accepting the limitations placed upon a particular standard when considering the broader context. It is imperative that one does not proceed in a situation haphazardly, without a thorough understanding of the underlying factors at play and the potential ramifications on the environment and individuals involved.

The subsequent procedures are as follows:

i. Characterize the conduct: Often, despite good and meticulously devised intentions, one becomes aware of the underlying manifestations associated with said conduct. When confronted with the emergence of detrimental repercussions from the course of action, it becomes imperative to acknowledge the necessity for change. It is imperative to provide precise details in delineating the conduct in order to ascertain the suitable course of action.

ii. Discern the element responsible for eliciting said behavior: Engaging in introspective analysis of one's emotions and past encounters in order to determine the underlying cause of said behavior. It is plausible that a fleeting or occasional psychological representation can engender stress or distort one's emotional state. It is advisable to approach the trigger with caution by firmly establishing a clear mental image, enabling a comprehensive understanding of the entire episode, including the underlying motivations behind said behavior.

iii. Distinguish the good intentions from the negative consequences of the behavior: Upon viewing the image, construct a comprehensive understanding and analyze the reasons behind the behavior's occurrence and its emergence. Consider solely the favorable outcomes initially brought forth by the plan and the corresponding negative ramifications associated with it. It is of paramount importance to maintain a positive attitude and ensure effective communication throughout the entire course of action. The individual ought to acquire an understanding of the constructive conduct, optimistic mindset, beneficial impact, and intended favorable consequences associated with said behavior. The elements that foster favorable intentions encompass self-preservation, safeguarding, and maintaining integrity. All of these factors endeavor to safeguard you from entering a state of vulnerability.

iv. Discover substitute options that possess an equivalent affirmative purpose, while refraining from fostering the adverse consequences associated with said conduct. It is imperative to identify an alternative that may manifest as an engaging pursuit, a mode of effective interpersonal engagement, or a cognitive process, all of which can aid in the avoidance of the undesirable inclination or behavior. It is advisable to consistently consider multiple alternatives and select the optimal one, with priority given to the most superior option. One should possess sufficient creativity and acquire an understanding of the positive impacts that the alternative option has on one's conduct and ultimate outcome.

v. Ensure the acceptance of the alternative by conducting an examination of all components: Assess the alternatives and identify the aspect that appears to be adversely affected by the initial flawed conduct. Inquire about the indications to ascertain whether the party consents to the alternative, or determine the need to seek fresh ones for approval.

vi. General consensus: It is imperative to extend approval to the various alternatives for each component. In the event that the component embraces the alternative, it would be prudent to contemplate the endorsement of other preexisting facets and elements of your being as well. Comprehensive endorsement should be given in consideration of the overall effect and expansion.

Task 10: Quieting The Internal Self-Critic

A multitude of individuals experience a decline in productivity and a negative impact on their emotional state as a result of the presence of their Inner Critic. The majority of individuals possess an inner voice, which can be bothersome as it delivers unconstructive and pessimistic thoughts to the individual's mind. The Inner Critic often expresses doubt in one's abilities or predicts unfavorable outcomes, discouraging any pursuit of self-improvement or efforts to better one's circumstances.

Naturally, maintaining an exclusively positive outlook on every situation and individual is not a prudent approach. It is imperative to adopt a realistic stance in order to mitigate imprudent risks and refrain from unwarranted optimism. Nonetheless, the Inner Critic is generally unproductive, and if we can pacify its influence, life is likely to become more fulfilling.

On subsequent occasions when you perceive the presence of that persistent inner voice, endeavor to undertake this particular exercise. To begin with, it is essential to be mindful of the manner in which your Inner Critic expresses itself. Does the voice belong to you, or is it the voice of another person? After a brief period of listening, envision the implementation of a sound filter or distinct audio manipulation, transforming the sound into a comical and high-pitched rendition. To what degree does this voice convey a sense of authority at present?

Give consideration to the precise origin of the voice. It is highly probable that you will perceive it as originating from the posterior region of your cranium. However, consider the possibility of envisioning it emanating from your pinky toe or your ankle, for instance. Doesn't the Inner Critic appear to have lost some of its credibility all of a sudden? Indeed, after envisioning your ankle providing you with purposeless negative thoughts, that inner voice will appear almost comical! The transformative power of imaginative visualization is truly remarkable.

NLP Applications In Professional, Parental, And Interpersonal Contexts

When you embark upon the implementation of the philosophy and techniques expounded in this literary work, significant transformations will manifest across all facets of your existence. In order to provide additional incentive and inspiration, this section will present a concise overview of how NLP can effectively assist individuals in domains such as work, parenting, and relationships.

NLP at Work

By acquiring the ability to quieten your internal evaluator, you will cultivate a heightened drive to undertake challenges, thus affording yourself an increased potential for accomplishment. Utilizing the confidence visualization technique has the potential to enhance your proficiency in situations where effectively conveying self-assurance is crucial, such as when delivering presentations to esteemed clients or senior executives. Reframing also holds immense value in one's professional realm, as it facilitates the transformation of negative feedback or situations formerly perceived as failures, thereby fostering a mindset conducive to learning and growth. This initiates a positive feedback loop whereby the acquisition of knowledge through feedback facilitates behavioral adaptation and eventual success in subsequent endeavors, leading to even more favorable feedback, continuing the cycle.

NLP and Parenting

There are two approaches to enhancing your parenting experience, namely the utilization of NLP techniques. Primarily, the strategies elucidated in this manual can be employed to enhance rapport, thereby fostering a more profound bond between oneself and one's children. One can employ the technique of pacing to diplomatically sway dispirited adolescents towards understanding their perspective, thus veering away from engaging in confrontational exchanges and disputes.

Furthermore, it is possible to impart these techniques directly to your children as well. For example, in the case of a child afflicted with low self-confidence, the Negative Belief Buster presents a readily acquired method to enhance their self-esteem. Should your offspring be grappling with anxiety issues, the Anchoring technique serves as a secure and user-friendly method to alleviate their distress, regardless of their location.

NLP and Relationships

By implementing the knowledge gained from this guide, your interpersonal connections are bound to experience enhanced outcomes. Presented herein are merely a few instances showcasing the various ways in which such occurrences may transpire. Suppose that you and your partner have recently engaged in more frequent arguments, surpassing the usual occurrence. This could be attributed to the significant stress you both have faced in your professional lives, leading to incessant quarrels concerning trivial matters such as the responsibility of taking out the trash. Utilizing the method of Dissociation, whereby assuming the perspective of an impartial observer, would greatly aid in mitigating the current circumstances.

An additional beneficial approach for individuals facing challenges in their relationships is known as the Whiteout. If you discover that you are persistently dwelling on past grievances or unpleasant memories, such as your partner's infidelity that occurred in the distant past, and these recurring mental images cause you distress, acquiring the ability to promptly suppress them can enable you to progress in life and concentrate on the current state of your relationship. Employing such methodologies enables one to transcend lingering resentment and trivial disputes.

If you happen to be unattached, it is important to note that NLP techniques can be instrumental in your endeavor to enhance your allure as a potential romantic companion. For example, individuals who possess confidence and feelings of assurance are generally perceived as being more aesthetically appealing. When you develop the ability to enhance your confidence and suppress your Inner Critic, this change will manifest in your daily conduct. If an individual finds themselves frequently attracting individuals who display neediness or negativity, they can anticipate a gratifying realization that enhancing their personal positivity will lead to a significant improvement in the quality of individuals they attract as potential companions. Please attempt the task and assess the outcomes.

Printed in the USA
CPSIA information can be obtained
at www.ICGtesting.com
LVHW010818160823
755278LV00013B/709